Keep/Discard

Keep/Discard

Poems by

Jacalyn Shelley

© 2025 Jacalyn Shelley. All rights reserved.
This material may not be reproduced in any form, published,
reprinted, recorded, performed, broadcast,
rewritten, or redistributed without
the explicit permission of Jacalyn Shelley.
All such actions are strictly prohibited by law.

Cover design by Shay Culligan
Cover image from iStock
Author photo by A.E. Tasoff

ISBN: 978-1-63980-743-7
Library of Congress Control Number: 2025937936

Kelsay Books
502 South 1040 East, A-119
American Fork, Utah 84003
Kelsaybooks.com

In memory of Jack and Beatrice Showell who

testify . . . and their relics . . . they comfort us through their mute witness, they're not allowing mortality to mean erasure . . .

—Kathryn Harrison, "What Remains"
The Writers Presence, 3rd Ed.

Flora Davis Showell, 1869–1945

Milton Showell, Sr., 1905–1934
Alma Jamison, 1907–1983
George V. Smith, 1876–1938
Alice Wells, 1895–1978

Milton (Jack) Showell, 1924–2016
Beatrice Wells, 1931–1991

Acknowledgments

Thank you to the following journals and digital platforms for publishing poems in this collection:

Aji Magazine: "Warning Light"
Awakenings Literary Review: "Artifacts of My Mother's Mania," "Ode to the Ceramic Jar"
BoomerLit: "My Father Tells Me About the 29th Anniversary Gift My Mother Gave Him"
Common Ground: "All of the Words of Jesus Are in Red"
Dunes Review: "Madonna of the Dry Tree"
Evening Street Review: "Why Does My Son Call Me?"
Main Street Rag: "Winter in Mind"
Misfit Magazine: "Terra Incognita," "Pussy Bow Blouse"
Penumbra: "My Father's Wallet," "Dance at Plumstead"
The Schuykill Valley Journal: "Keep/Discard," "There, There Traveler"
Shot Glass Journal: "Three Gloves"
Thirteen Myna Birds: "In Kansas, She Swings," "My Grandfather Milton at the Hunting Club, 1934"
Two Hawks Quarterly: "Like Cordelia"

And thank you to my Leap Street Poetry family: Deborah Bayer, Shelley Cohen, Barbara Daniels, Cole Eubanks, and Ben Hyland.

Contents

Aperture	11
Like Cordelia	13
Terra Incognita	14
In Kansas, She Swings	16
Pussy Bow Blouse	17
Artifacts of My Mother's Mania	19
Beach Haven	22
Winter in Mind	24
Salvation Army Thrift Store	26
Madonna of the Dry Tree	27
Three Gloves	29
My Father Tells Me About the 29th Anniversary Gift My Mother Gave Him	30
My Father's Wallet	31
Keep/Discard	32
Dance at Plumstead	33
My Grandfather Milton at the Hunting Club, 1934	35
Alma: The Name Spoken Once	37
My Great-Grandmother Flora's Book	39
All of the Words of Jesus Are in Red	40
Warning Light	41
You Are My Clay Grandmother	42
My Mother's Marginalia	44
What Falls	45
Washington's Tent	46
Why Does My Son Call Me?	47
First Apartment	49
There, There Traveler	51

Aperture

I wonder if I knew what was going on,
        did I hear cries like this before and thought
                feline not catbird.

Although I studied the leafing out
        of oak trees, did I pay enough
                attention to the pitch pines

hidden behind them?
        Dad kept the ledger of
                our lives according to

rules I couldn't decipher.
        When I transgressed he
                glowered at me as if

I was a star-nosed mole.
        Faceless. Mom
                photographed our lives,

created a gallery of smiles
        festooned around our home.
                Looking into the lens

of her camera, I held her
        at the center of my life.
                After her car crash,

the accounting began.
        First subtraction:
                the scent of Chanel #5

mingled with smoke
  twisting up from
    her cigarettes that dropped

stars on our clothes.
  Later, division
    of her stack of hats.

I didn't claim the floppy
  brown suede or the one
    covered in daisies. I chose

the gray wide brim hat
  to block the savage light.
    Patterns crack, provide

an aperture for understanding
  like the photos of my teenage Mom
    sitting on the broken steps

at her childhood home,
  and Dad's joyful face
    as he carried me on his shoulders.

What is the history of grief?
  Peripheral like fog, it conceals
    then lifts to expose the limbs of trees.

Like Cordelia

      if I were a good daughter,
maybe I could've told my father
he was *Dearer than eyesight,*

      as Goneril did. If I obeyed
the fifth commandment, I thought
that would be enough. For his ears

      my tongue should have sung
Daddy, you are the best father in the world,
words my sister wrote on the wallet-sized

      photograph Dad kept in his desk.
Perhaps she pressed her cheek into his hand
as she gave him her picture, sealing his eyes

      with her hot touch of affection.
Had I smelled a fault? After she took
his house, and all the good jewelry, my arms

      carried home the cardboard box
of jumbled things—torn towels that once
wiped rain off Dad's face, a steel watch

      that pinched his wrist, and a cell phone
now mute to my message: *Have you nothing
to say?* Nothing from his blue lips.

Terra Incognita

Because Boris the cockatoo elicits compassion
sitting alone in a steel cage,

because the blue lids that surround
his black eyes look exotic,

and he dances to the beat of Queen's
"Another One Bites the Dust,"

my friends ask, *How can you put him
in a cage?* Does he dream of koalas,

kangaroos, the blood-red boulders
in the Rainbow Valley as my father did?

Dad told me, *I want to go there,*
one finger pointed south and west

before his hands danced down his chest,
his arms, his legs as if he were painting

aboriginal white dashes and dots
on his body, as if he could breathe in

sunrise in the bush. Boris asks,
How ya doin'? like the pharmacy tech,

who, after handing me medicine says,
There you go, just like Boris,

in a voice identical to mine as I drop
a chicken bone into his metal dish.

After I drench Boris's white feathers
in my shower, he flaps his wings

scattering droplets, his black tongue
loosens and he whistles "Ode to Joy."

Why didn't Dad open the travel book
I gave him? When Boris comes out

of his cage he surveys my small rooms,
rappels back to his perch. He rests his head

between his flightless wings and
one unblinking eye stares at me.

In Kansas, She Swings

open the car door,
tells my father,
*I can't take this
anymore.*

At home my mother's
Limoges vase. Lip and
foot trimmed in gold.
A stem held upright
in its midnight blue
belly. Wild roses.

Her hands grapple
with a rolling pin,
and she rows and rows
and again she rows
her dough out into
an ocean. She dives
into brackish lagoons.

It's her thyroid,
my father says.
Sometimes,
it's easier to blame
an internal organ.

Pussy Bow Blouse

It was my mother,
no, it was Margaret
Thatcher who thought
her pussy bow blouses
were *soft & sweet,*
not unlike the flamboyant
pink bodice worn by
A Liberated Woman.
One arm extends across
the canvas as if to say
*Look. Here. I am
smoking a cigarette.*

I don't remember when
my mother gave me
my paisley blouse
with puffy sleeves,
cinched cuffs
& two thin ribbons
to tie a modest bow.
She might have called it
a secretary's shirt,
but I wore mine with
navy blue pants,
not a skirt.

It was in Altoona,
no, it was in Erie, where
the office manager
called me *Hon.*
Maybe I wasn't joking
with him when I said,
*Back at the home office
they call me Attila the Hun.*
There is little doubt
he laughed, much like

the 47th President caught on
video tape. Yes, he did say,
*You can grab them by
the pussy.* Labia majora.
Labia minora. Folds of flesh.
Folds of fabric. My pussy bow blouse.
Perfect in its fit.

Artifacts of My Mother's Mania

Let me stand again in the too-sweet scent
of hyacinth, let this desire
to dance find the arms
of a lemon-bright forsythia,
so I might wear
my mother's fire opal
ablaze on my finger,
her garnets the size
of pomegranate seeds strung
as a necklace,

the same jazz berry & red-orange
colors of the buildings
in Mom's watercolor landscape.
The World Trade Center's
spire isn't penned
with ink but shadow,
the windows a wash of
canary not sunglow,
& the struts
not of silver, but of timber wolf,

a color similar to the charcoal
palette Mom used
to draw Christ
& all his crosses
after the priest pronounced
her repainting of the saints—
Mary, Peter, Anthony—
too bright.

And here, because it's still April,
bitter sweet leaves
flee the woods,
clatter toward a paddock
lined with wire.
A chestnut mare raises
her head like a tulip.
If her snout touches the steel
will she feel, will she ask,
as my mother did,
What did I do?

What does a child know of her parent's
struggle? Perhaps only the
constant & elaborate
preparations for feast days,
holidays, birthdays,
the change of curtains
to mark each season, each
day of the week the same meal.

Sometimes when we danced in the kitchen
she would sing "tea for two
& two for tea." Her voice
would soften & her body
would tremble
as if she were
a soft wooden plant
bent by an unrelenting breeze.

Tomorrow I will visit those saints,
the smoky candlelight
settling at their feet, a light
her gold bracelet
will catch as it kisses
my wrist, warms the amber
garland clasped at
the nape of my neck,
hangs across the purple
veins of my breasts.

Beach Haven

My mother raked the bones
        of ospreys & gulls, the shells
                of clams & oysters, & the skeletons
                      of crabs from the bay sediment

dredged to create my parents' land.
        To plant tomatoes, cucumbers
                & peppers, she filled my father's
                      work boots with the crystalline soil.

She thought the brown, green & red
        garden lovely in a disorderly way.
                What remains at the front
                      of their house is the evergreen scent

of bayberry clumps she scalped
        from the sand dunes. For my daily
                use are the things most precious—
                      an ice cream scoop with a worn red handle,

her spoon-scratched mixing bowls
        for making date nut bread & blueberry
                muffins, & the two-legged colander,
                      dented by a scalding pot as it released

its pasta. Tonight, I will gnaw
        on the bones of the dead as the sky
                passes from light to dark & Boris
                      will squawk & squawk until

he settles down to sleep.
      He presses one claw up &
            into his heart feathers
                      as the other claw grips his perch.

Winter in Mind

In one story, the father holds his child
on his shoulders, helps her face

a bitter wind, and in another story,
the father stares at a blue-lit screen,

reads the news, plays video games.
In one story, the father and daughter

fish together. Their hands touch
as each invisible line is set into a river.

And in another story, the father shakes
dice, drinks beer, gives his daughter

money to ride roller coasters.
But in this story the father reads

to his daughter, the smell of calf hide
on their hands. She pulls at the fold-

out page. Into the starry heaven three
trains travel along railroad tracks

to the Sun, the Moon and Mars.
After her father dies, does she think

some attendant from the locomotive
of heaven took him away?

He leaves her this *First Book
of Knowledge* where the thick black

strokes of his fountain pen scraped
into the frontispiece: *To Beatrice*

on her 2nd Birthday, Father.
He leaves her other books of heft

and impenetrability. Books written
with winter in mind. Beneath

his dedication, her childhood scrawl:
I love my father with all my heart.

Salvation Army Thrift Store

With the kiss of touch,
my father raised from his bag
plaid of socks & striped of pants,
buttons for coats & zippers for skirts.
Atop his fist sat
my mother's pill-box hat.
You are greatly shaken,
a woman said.
Sit here and eat this bread.
How wiped clean were my mother's
stones & turquoise ring
by the woman's cloth.
My father thought he saw someone,
though no one else was there
whose silver earrings
swept the side of her neck
& he heard my mother's laughter.

Madonna of the Dry Tree

*after my grandmother Alice's statuette
of her and my mother*

Who can find
        its end? My hair bound

in a knot
        at the nape of my neck

loops in
        upon itself. To calm

your wavering
        fists, I put a ball in your

Christ—
        you-cry-all-the-time hands.

Perhaps if I rested
        my nose on the soft bones

of your head
        I could smell bliss.

On the edge
        of my knees I hold you

a reckless
        distance from my breast.

After you
        were cut away from me,

marked by
        a belly knot,

Ann the whittler
        chiseled us out of

a dark wood,
        confined you and me

between parallel lines
        of a straight-backed chair.

Three Gloves

Yesterday it snowed. Your brown gloves slid
        off the shelf, and I remembered you
ice skating. How each leg crossed over the other,

the setting down of each foot, the circles you sketched
        on the frozen cranberry bog. But here's this
one black glove. The slack leather bulges where you wore

your Masonic ring. Your handshake, a test—
        those who could bear the hard
squeeze and those who could not. After I kissed

your dry forehead, I crumpled into my brother's arms.
        We recalled your strange love,
the moments your hand seemed disconnected.

Didn't you run to our cribs to hear us breathe?
        The dead are helpless in our hands.
Last week I sensed you were here behind the screen door.

My Father Tells Me About the 29ᵗʰ Anniversary Gift My Mother Gave Him

Perhaps if your mother had her own money
she would've purchased something new—
a necktie in burgundy, my favorite color,
a watch with a fine leather band. She
selected from a box of notecards Derain's
woodcut of *Grangousier,* a man wearing
a burgundy robe and a studded wrist band.

You are a woman with her own money,
our little girl who, when I gave you
the chance to pick up acorns for a penny
a piece, knelt, counted to four hundred
and ninety-nine before I could stop you.

After I pulled the silk bow, unwrapped
the lavender linen from her gift, I said,
*Yes. Let me hang it in our living room.
Here near the door,* where it remained
beyond the years of your mother's life,
my second marriage, until I moved it
next to my bed in the nursing home.

Out of that box of cards, your mom
could've chosen any rogue—cyclops,
the gambler, a warrior knight, but she
chose the man with a lusty appetite
for his wife, a king with a good heart.

My Father's Wallet

My brown leather hide folds and unfolds for you.
I wish you would fill my crevices with dollars.

Endlessly. That your fingers would pull the paper
skeletons into the living room light. Give allowances.

I crave holding one curve of your body, the skin
how many women knew? Sitting next to the blonde

secretary, you plucked your family out of my photo-pleats,
accordion of mute music, cracks in the earth's brittle crust.

Keep/Discard

When, after my mother burnt the lasagna,
after my father remarked, *You've burnt*

our dinner again! Mom rose from the table,
asked me *Want to go to the beach?* No one

could swim the ocean like my mother.
I watch her feet drown in the sandy bottom,

her shoulders dip under the waves.
Her head bobs up and her body sinks

into the rhythmic reaching strokes of a languid
crawl. Breathing is all that matters.

Unlike me. I pose, worship the sun, walk
the line between dry and wet, pick up shells.

Which is better? Keep. Discard. I cannot float.
I hold my head high, jerking from side to side.

Why couldn't Dad just eat around the burnt edges?
She emerges out of the calmed sea into the pink-

purple evening glow. Her shoulders chrome shiny,
a sprig of seaweed in her hair. *Ready to go home?*

I'm astonished at my parents' cleaving
to their own secret language of love. He offers

her a bowl brimming with rum-raisin ice cream.
They nestle together on the couch.

Dance at Plumstead

*after my grandmother Alice's statuette of
her dancing with George*

Nose to nose they breathed
      the same breath,

spoke the silent language
      of overheated molecules.

To "The Rustle of Spring,"
      his knees dipped,

his pelvis pressed against
      her skirt, freed

her foot from the ground.
      She felt

like a wisteria vine
      embracing an oak,

a kind of faith written
      in an unsanctioned

script. But he spoke with
      a different placement

of the lips, the tongue, conjured
      himself a cloud

wandering between horizons.
      Didn't Ann whittle

them from the same block of wood,
        salvaged from

the Valley of Ashes? After he died,
        he left her nothing

but the imprint of his body,
        three children,

and *The Book of Musical Knowledge.*
        She tried to unravel

the song of the once breathing
        trees, how their leaves

swirled, how their twigs dropped
        notes into a pool.

My Grandfather Milton at the Hunting Club, 1934

A doe dangled from her hind legs
        on your right, a buck on your left,
                shotgun in your hand.

You glared at the photographer
        as if he accused you of something
                terrible. There's guilt enough

in everyone's life
        to account for a look like that.
                Dark suit, tie loosened,

your left hand tucked
        inside your pants pocket. Are you
                thinking what to reply?

Did the camera catch you peering
        into the future? Your body mangled
                under a motorcycle.

You told your nine-year-old son
        you were his brother. The story
                he tells of the day your coffin

was lifted off the kitchen table
        is about your white parrot
                who said *Milton,* bowed his head

and died a week later. Your mother
 slipped your photograph inside
  a thin tin frame that hung over

your son's desk
 for the rest of his life.
  Like him I study your shadowed face.

Alma: The Name Spoken Once

i.

i held him in this room
              this room red & burning

to leave him was not easy
              after we were no longer

blind to one another
              after my arms held his weight

his small wrinkled hand
              gripping my finger

held in this room
              this room papered in roses

ii.

i was given a new name
              jack   short for jackson hospital

there were whispers
              questions about the color

of my parents' hair
              never mentioned was her name

until the day
              i enlisted in the army

then my brother, Milton
>   became my father Milton,

then moments
>   like those between lightning

& its sound
>   in the yellow kitchen where she left me

My Great-Grandmother Flora's Book

After I stood at attention on a narrow ledge,
next to Dickens or Twain or the encyclopedias,

one of Flora's great-granddaughters pulled
the tip of my spine, nestled me on her belly.

My binding splayed open to breathe
the fragrance of one fly-swirl day in July

when Flora placed the shattered wildflower
at the story of the "International Jewel Hunter."

Inside my front cover, she tickled me
repeatedly with the practiced writing of her name.

Once she tattooed me with red and blue pencils.
Who was she thinking of? Sometimes

I wish I could have read Flora as she read me.
Even today I hear the scrape of her thumbnail

creating the indelible creases at the corners
of two pages to mark the poems "The Farmer

Feeds All" and "The Sower." Those pointy folds
remind me of her dog Fritz's ears. Flora read to

her grandson every day until the day
he could read, and in his excitement

his hands smeared huckleberry jam on
my pages. I had never tasted sweetness before.

All of the Words of Jesus Are in Red

Given with love, his black leather Bible,
        rubbed gray by his fingers,
records no marriages, no baptisms,

only a strip of paper placed at the beginning
        of Lamentations. How do I know
which passages gave my father solace?

One thin black ribbon crosses
        a New Testament page.
Only the words of Jesus are in red.

Only my father's second bride could tell me
        that my father loved me.
I said to my first husband, *I am*

a resounding gong. To the man whose child
        I miscarried, I wrote,
Love never fails. When we are shaken,

we set to work. After his second wife died,
        my father wrote his family history
on hundreds of yellow-lined pages.

Are we not bound to the same plot?
        Now, like a child,
I scrawl his many names.

Warning Light

In the torrential rain
my check engine light flashes on
like my father suddenly awake
in his wheelchair staring at
the green Formica table,
another day of eating pea puree,
mashed potatoes and Spam,

England's rain thrashing
against him as he trudges
to his tent-office
past the C47s and gliders.

But he's drinking Kool-Aid
looking at a gray locked door.
Where is he now?
Maybe taking that snapshot of

the girl on the beach, the Channel
at her back, the place where
a plane could slip into the gunmetal sea
as easily as a letter
into an envelope.

You Are My Clay Grandmother

after my grandmother Alice's clay jar circa 1880

fern green color,
        stout, substantial
        with a chipped lid.

From gray riverbank sludge
        you could've been made
        into russet bricks,
        rough to the touch

but easily bound with mortar
        to create something
        bigger than yourself.
        What are the dreamy

aspirations of mud? To be
        the two cuneiform
        tablets written on by
        the hand of God,

or blue roof tiles whose eyes
        to the heavens
        show the stars
        the stars. Something

made, can it ask its maker,
        Why this shape?
        Why this purpose?
        Porcelain parrots rest

on my shelf. They remind me
> of you saying,
> *Dance like a bird.*
> I was never what

we hoped I would be. Now,
> you stand next to a book
> whose cover is a girl
> in ballet class

that might remind you of me.
> She wears a white tutu,
> and her hair is pinned back
> to tame her curls.

My Mother's Marginalia

She was the master of the green or black underline,
just in case there might be a reason to remember

an idea or thought. But if my mother didn't agree,
she scrawled her points of debate down the page.

She would also assign stars. In her musty college
literature book, Donne, Pope, Auden and Frost

were rated one star. Whitman received eight
and a bold *I love this!*

When I saw she had trouble spelling the same word
I struggle with, I laughed. There on the blank last page

of the anthology *rhythm* was written nine times.
I turn my mother's bracelet round and round

my wrist when I need reminding that whatever
is being lived now will not persist forever. Still

I won't carry her *Book of Common Prayer* with me
to church as she would've wanted. Its cover red

as the blood she shed in the car where she died.
This book, lying in the passenger's seat, had

a simple strand of maroon yarn doubled over
to mark perhaps the last words she read:

Lord Almighty grant us a peaceful night
and a perfect end.

What Falls

I behold the slate-colored juncos
landing beneath the feeder, trace
the droppings of mice cracking
my house open as crickets grieve.
Into the evening I step to catch
sassafras hands the colors of wild
strawberries, dandelions, orange
sunsets, as if God threw confetti
to celebrate this day. The sun
loses some of its power.
The rain no longer drips from
branches forsaken by their leaves.
Their wrists thin as winter, thin
as my mother's. Her voice now
a loose trill of song fading into
brown-needled trees. Feeding
on the ground, the juncos take
what falls to them.

Washington's Tent

after Washington's War Tent
Museum of the American Revolution

          now a sacred relic
of the republic after a grandson
snipped pieces for souvenirs,
after it was sold to fund aid for
Confederate widows.

          When I'm a widow,
I will soothe my private sadness
with every walnut scented opening
of the silverware box my husband made.

          We are living in
tents again. Near Bastogne
& I'm writing by candlelight.
Written by an Army nurse
to my father. Words spared from
a dumpster's dark belly.

          From the chaos
of objects I've collected, who will
discover the clay vessel marked
Xios—a whistle whose spout
touched my lover's lips.

          And the rosary beads
strung by a friend that hang within
reach of my bed. Where will they
be found? A Goodwill store. Or held
in the hands of a son of a grandson.

Why Does My Son Call Me?

My son asks, *How's your other son?*
which means, *How's Boris?*
my pet cockatoo, a dinosaur born
out of the oldness of the world.

I pour water into a stainless bowl,
drop almonds in another. He toddles
up to me, mirrors my swaying back
and forth before he lowers his head
for me to tousle his yellow crown.

Who understands what caring for
another creature fully entails?

My son's ear presses against his phone,
listens as I speak of long days filled
with daily chores, going to stores,
teaching Boris how to speak English,
how to whistle Beethoven's "Fifth"
and "Hava Nagila." After Boris shreds
pages from *The New York Times*
that line his cage, he translates
my deep evening sighs into
a low growl.

Boris asks in a voice identical
to mine, *How ya doin'?* then
answers, *All right, Mr. Bird,*
as if to reassure us that someday
my son will treasure the oldness
of our world—Tolstoy, Mussorgsky

and Boris—maybe out of fondness
for the resonance of my voice.
But one day my little dinosaur
may echo my son's speech,
whistle his songs. If my son
listens to his own voice
will he know his inheritance?

First Apartment

You stop at the white lacquered dresser
        stenciled with buttercups entwined around
                acanthus drawer pulls. Over the objects

you want me to see, your finger points
        to the Angel Wings and Baby's Ear shells
                I sent from Florida and the teak comb

your grandfather engraved with your name.
        Your hand skitters past a pack of Marlboros
                I prefer not to think about. Slipped inside

the mirror's edges are photographs
        of people I don't recognize except
                the snapshot of your parents—

your mother before she died
        and my son. I catch a glimpse of you
                more beautiful than I have ever been.

Your arms tattooed with flowers
        running down the trellis of your body
                ending in bouquets at each knee.

Before you move away toward
        the baritone call for more coffee,
                the Queen Anne looking glass captures

your curly hair brushing against mine.
        You may not know this: In the roots
                of your hair, no matter the dye you color

the shafts, there are centuries
      of grandparents cheering for you,
            some in different languages from the one

you speak. Remember: I'm listening for
      the two-syllable word—Granny! The person
            who will fly to you when you cry out in the dark.

There, There Traveler

                              ticket in hand.
Your trunk trails behind you.
Ready to board? Back to your father's town.

Tug, tug the train pulls you as if by your tongue.
Your father's been dead ten years. Still, you taste soap
in your twice-washed mouth.

Too, too much turmoil here in the touring coach
as thousands of tunes thrum. You eat like your father—
three salted tomato slices and chicken tenders—

fret like him too, about taboos and tabulations,
tambourines and night trains, ask the twilight engineer,
Where's the fuel stored?

You're safe, he says, *It's in the tender car lined with tin.*
He offers you a peach out of his tattered pocket,
and you take from him as if he's your father—

at times terrified for you, at times the titan of thunder
rumbling along the tracks of your life.

About the Author

Keep/Discard is Jacalyn Shelley's first poetry collection. Her poems have been widely published in journals such as *The Comstock Review* and *The Schuylkill Journal*. She's also been published in several anthologies like *Welcome to the Resistance: Poetry as Protest* and was nominated for four Pushcart Poetry prizes.

Her teachers and mentors include Stephen Dunn, Kathleen Graber, Peter Murphy, Emari DiGiorgio, and Barbara Daniels. As a member of the South Jersey Poets Collective, Jackie participates in poetry readings in Atlantic City and hosts the Leap Street Poets Workshop. She lives in the Pinelands of New Jersey with her husband Alan and Boris their pet cockatoo.

Connect with Jackie and follow her work at:
jacalynshelley.com

www.ingramcontent.com/pod-product-compliance
Lightning Source LLC
Chambersburg PA
CBHW031206160426
43193CB00008B/527